The Ledger of Mistakes

Also by Kathy Nelson

Cattails (chapbook)
Whose Names Have Slipped Away (chapbook)

The Ledger of Mistakes

Kathy Nelson

Terrapin Books

Terrapin Books
4 Midvale Avenue
West Caldwell, NJ 07006

www.terrapinbooks.com

ISBN: 978-1-947896-64-2
Library of Congress Control Number: 2023936169

First Edition

Cover art by Catrin Welz-Stein
Precious Flight
Digital artwork
www.catrinwelzstein.com

Cover Design by Diane Lockward

Contents

And These Old Mountains   3

    I

Eclipse   7
Boundary I   8
February   9
Doily   10
The Last Thing She Ever Said to Me   12
Electra Contemplates Justice   13
The Arsonist   14
Easter, 1956   15

    II

Pot Liquor   19
Cake   20
Unsummoned   21
How to Unknot a Straitjacket   22
Dead Five Years   23
Our Lady of the Locked Unit   24
Mercy   25
I Never Thought My Mother   26

    III

809 Whitehall Road, Knoxville, Tennessee   31
Rondelet: Electra at Twenty   32
Rivals   33
Did You Know Azalea Honey's
    Poisonous, Like Guilt?   34
My father just home   36
My Mother Wants to Know If Her
    Money's Holding Out   38

Another Buoyancy   40
Electra at the River I   42
Under the Canopy of Night   44
Turtles, Late Summer   45
Revision   46

IV

Piano Lesson Triolet   51
At the Least Movement, the Whole
    Structure Collapses   52
Mother of Roses   54
A Plane Rises, Smaller, Smaller,
    into Clouds   56
Burn Maybe Bones   58
Lilacs   59
Maestro   60
Electra at the River II   61
Boundary II   62
Snakes   63

V

Electra at Seventy   67
Landscape with Ash   68
Enough   70
Taco Tuesday   71
The Potted Jade   72
Quantum Physics   73
Forty-Ninth Year of a Marriage   74
Boundary III   75
Cahokia   76
The Last Dust Swept Away   78
Lunaria   79

Acknowledgments   81
About the Author   83

for Nora and Fran

And These Old Mountains

Why remember the dead? Why finger
like prayer beads their hurts, hungers,
all I could never give them? The earth
buries its bones in ash, leaves them
layered along channels of cut rock,
hidden within the Precambrian folds.

Daisies, lanky and exuberant, are waving
like children, sun splashing their faces.
The pine sheds light like water; a hawk
churns over the valley on an updraft.
Across the sky's blue sea, a cloud sails.
Soon it will all be forgotten—

the hawk, the daisies, my mother
and the rich black soil from which she
dug the green stalks to bring them to me,
something that would keep on living,
and the curving highway carved from schist,
the winding tunnels that separated us—

I

Eclipse

The landscape stitched with fencerows,
aflame with crepe myrtle, the trees lush and reaching,
I loved the road to the rural hospital. I loved

the corridor, my footsteps whispering from the elevator,
and the stately ceremony: stand still, erect, like a petitioner,
before the words *Gero-Psych Unit*, press the bell,
count my breaths until someone unlocks the door.

The unhurried rhythms of voices, the nurse's serene smile,
the dozen or so gray brethren dozing on davenports, recliners,
or shuffling, unperturbed, along hallways,

my mother blinking, placid, on the sofa,
her brow as smooth as an innocent's.

The doctor's low drone intoning the subtle balance
between mania and depression, the abacus of dosages—
Depakote, Lexapro.

When I slid alongside her, we were like feuding neighbors
gazing up at the eclipsed moon, forgetting all of it
under the blazing darkness. I loved my mother's astonishment
then, and her curious regard—a baby's—at such intimacy

with a stranger. And because I knew she'd been disarmed,
I loved enfolding her, as though after long absence,
and kissing the marble of her cheeks, forehead, each eyebrow,
over and over, while the barrier, long ago erected, crumbled.

Boundary I

In midday heat, under a tree-high pavilion, a giraffe wraps
its tongue around romaine leaves offered one by one—
Audri explains (at nine the world's ambassador): it feels
something like the cat's sandpaper, something like her
slippery own. That length of muscle lashing toward my
darling's hand! When she was five, I trembled seeing her
gently stroke—two small fingers—a yellow snake. Meerkats,
crocodiles, okapis—she leads us, her grandparents; when we
stop to read the plaques, she shuttles between us, a border
collie among dallying sheep.

A thousand shames
ago, I lay evenings in a hammock, pale light winking
through the mantle of leaves above me, lightning bugs
blinking, TV light seeping through the window where my
mother and father watched the news, and I listened to the
moon and the frogs called and the katydids ticked and a
million molecules amassed into a nearness so large my skin
prickled and my edges began to dissolve into the rising dark.

February

Whereas jonquils bloom yellow and Christmas lights
dangle—unlit, anemic—from the gutter,

and the rain-mirrored porch wears the bare trees,
and circles ripple out, one not quite gone

as the next drop bull's-eyes the water. Whereas
Cane Creek spills over its banks and slides

across the road. And the four crows that settled yesterday
in the top of the sycamore to twitch their tail feathers

and chatter to each other have not returned. And the storm
door rattles, useless. And the ink bottle waits,

obliging, for the dry nib. Whereas my parents
lie on a hill overlooking I-40 two hours west.

And the bag she thrust at me—her sentences huffing
with scold, her lines end-stopped—inside, embroidery.

You'll have to finish this. I'm unable.
It reads *My Daughter, My Shining Star,* the slate gray

thread stuttering around one pansy, languishing.
Her needle, trailing green, still stuck in the linen.

Doily

no idle twiddle but a worry of thumbs a whirring
      pad over nail over pad behind the little wall

of Aunt Winnie's interlaced fingers her movie star
      lacquered nails the only thing about her

that wasn't plain the ample body the broad forearms
      the homemade dress she sat beside me coaxing

that's it pull through the loop and snug it up
      chain slip stitch half-double crochet across the room

Jesus' flaming bleeding thorn-wrapped heart shone
      from a frame how could a child not ponder suffering

the thread in my fumbling fingers turned to chaos
      she gently freed my hands sweet-talked the mess

danced the hook first one way then the other
      showing me again my goodness a given imagine

the threat to my mother with her list of improvements
      it didn't matter whether I was nice cute smart

thin pretty charming fun-to-be-around Aunt Winnie
    filled my cup with sugar and milk tinged

with a splash of bitter coffee to heighten the sweet
    she sorted her crochet hooks by size so do I

The Last Thing She Ever Said to Me

I caught her before she fell.

She laughed then, *What would I do without you?*
Kept strolling, sweeping her arm toward dogwood blossoms
terraced along the limbs—a conductor before the bow
acknowledging the white-robed children's choir.

Or she never fell at all but sighed out of her body
into that light weaving through the leaves of trees.

No wheelchair, no surgery, no nightmares
where I tortured her, refused to take her home, no
You won't have to bother with me anymore—you must be so proud,
the little line of her heartbeat bouncing steady across the screen.

She never grew old.

No scraping her walker along the hallway,
calling my name as I strode, no, bolted ahead of her escaping.

That card—calico kitten draped over the head of a St. Bernard,
This made me smile and I thought of you. Love, Mother.

I learned not to study the mirror
for the slope of her cheekbone.

Electra Contemplates Justice

after *Electra at the Tomb of Agamemnon*
—Sir Frederic Lord Leighton

Alone, too young for sorrow, she cradles her head
between her arms. Twin to the marble column
beside her, her robe's folds cold as the dead
father her faithless mother's already forgotten.

Electra had knelt beside him, his body warm
against her hand and cheek, she'd matched
his stillness bone for bone. A fissure tore
inside her, hot and jagged vengeance hatched.

The gods neglect Justice, leave it to starve
on its fraying rope. Only she to unleash
its muscled haunches. Her mother will struggle hard
against the fatal claws of her righteous grief.

Now together, in cold earth they'll lie.
No one to remember either but I.

The Arsonist

At home, she used to crank the stove to high,
walk away, leave the potatoes to boil dry,

then char hard as bricks, the kitchen dimming
with smoke as she thumbed her magazines.

At the lunch table in the new place, she hectors
the ladies, their soup spoons stalled, midair—

She'll set the building on fire one night as they sleep.
She'll laugh as they burn. It's a promise.

Her words flare to ash until all she can do
is gape like a lost child at the conflagration.

She squirrels her jewelry, stashes her money, her keys.
What are you doing going through my things?

(Someone is trying to kill her.) In the locked unit,
she walks the halls, pulls the fire alarm,

presses her ear to the door, insatiable for sirens.

Easter, 1956

The magnolia blossoms in the wallpaper behind us,
    her straw cloche scattered with lilacs. My face shines

        in the flash. Stiff organza, netted rosebud headband.
    My mother tilts her head toward me, smiling.

I slide the photo from its frame again to see her hand
    reaching, the way my hem drapes across her fingers.

        Not so much restraining as inviting, coaxing me
    to defer escape from the camera frame. Not quite

forbearance, not quite melancholy. Once, in a dream,
    I awoke from numb forgetting, remembered —

        oh, the longing — a daughter I'd never known,
    lost in the night. On the horizon, beacons shone,

but I stumbled in a canyon of talus slopes and boulders.
    I never had the dream again and it's just as well.

        A person could be destroyed by such hopelessness.
    I have been my mother and I have been my daughter.

I have driven slowly along a curb cajoling
    my girl — *honey, please get back in* — and I have

raced along a corridor, a walker scraping behind me,
a plaintive voice calling my name. I've lied and I've

been the one lied to, the advocate and the adversary,
the swatter and the fly, the witness and the one

afraid to look. I have shrunk from the cliff's edge,
and I have marveled at the possibilities of flight.

II

Pot Liquor

Not the crystal, not the Murano paperweights,
not the Hummels she'd accused me of coveting.

What I brought home, the last dust swept
from my mother's place—that little Madonna

of generosity, glass shaker, octagonal base,
domed chrome screw-top. The white sifting

so perfectly, neither fast nor slow, the only one
in the kitchen that never clogs—for breakfast eggs,

the slice of tomato.
                    I go on reaching for it.
The reluctance of water to boil or freeze as salt

is added. The heart's narrow tolerance—too much,
pressure builds, too little, the pulse flutters.

Shimmer of oil, of onion, sliced half-moons—
collards simmered all afternoon with bone.

Cake

The strawberry cake on my plate—curlicues
of frosting, tender layers pink as cheeks
on prom night—makes promises it can't keep.

       The problem with getting what you think
          you want is living with it. Same as not getting
             what you want. Two sources of suffering.

Just once my mother said, as if reciting,
as if she'd practiced, *don't know what I'd do
without you,* then straightened, shrank away.

       But then there's getting what you don't want:
          *their pills, their poison puddings, know-nothings
            calling my name, telling me what to do,*

*and then there's my so-called daughter,
the goody-goody, stealing the ring he gave me.*
Quickest of a thousand ways to suffer? Crave.

Unsummoned

my mother pleads

from the bardo

she misses her body   its fevered purring

its fleshy rhythms

heft and substance

she's nowhere now

the lost lie down   she says   among their bodies

none get back in

(I think of how)   she slips   unsummoned

through crevices

soaks into my tissues

gone now

she inhabits me—   her loneliness

as I reach for a shirt

How to Unknot a Straitjacket

Take the photo of your mother off the wall.
Let the blood drain. (Don't use a chalice.)

Make a list
of the treasons you've earned.

Wreathe them around your neck like skulls.

Map the patterns of need in the copperhead's scales,
remembering her seductive charm.

Count the times you ate cake sitting alone in your car—
the barbaric crumbs, the sticky plastic fork,
the box sagging in the footwell.

Reread your instructions to yourself—
Do Not Rescue, Do Not Suffer.

Put at the top of the list of remains:
the sound of her voice in your throat.

Dead Five Years

I sat beside her, the damp cloth drying
on the little oven of her forehead,
watered with a straw the withered flower
of her mouth, considered a pillow, perhaps
a thumb, a forefinger, a palm across
her mouth and nose.
                              Who would know?
The hospice nurse ordered me to go,
and I wandered with the somnambulists,
studied the calligraphed names on the doors.
Still, she breathed like a machine,
something loose, wet grinding in there.

When she copied and recopied her new
address, coercing her ruined brain to learn—
slips of paper under the sofa, in her pockets,
among her shoes. When she followed me
like a child, afraid of being left behind.
When she gave up trying to turn on the TV.
When she grieved,
                I worked hard all my life
and now I have to ask you for my money.
When she hijacked the tai chi class.
When she said,
                You got what you've been waiting for
just before she closed her eyes and tried to die.

Our Lady of the Locked Unit

From the valley of the shadow (Haldol, Risperidone), my mother
wakes, happy as a warbler in pine forest. She's forgotten how to walk
but stands from her wheelchair, teeters like a baby bird perusing air,
or like Rodin's Old Courtesan, or like the cripple at Capernaum.

This would be a story about miracles if it weren't so full of sorrow.
Instead, I'll call it Transfiguration.

Hello, Beautiful! she sings out
to the CNA. To the med Tech, *I love you!* No matter her serrated
syllables, he's always cooed *darlin', perfect,* kissing her cheek,
slipping Valium-laced vanilla pudding between her teeth.

In the dread-crippled, arthritic, word-terminal, decay-doomed room,
the lunch tray clatter slows and a line forms—the beleaguered faithful
gather for the Holy Mother's blessing. And I, her famished acolyte,
don't I ache too for that beneficence?

Good morning!
her bony palms unfold the maintenance man's blameless hand.

Mercy

She listed in her wheelchair, a castaway
on a wrecked man-of-war. I knelt before her,
as if to beg, struggling—pull up the sagging sock,
wrestle the swollen foot into the new shoe—
stiff tongue, sluggish cotton against padded heel.
My mother said—

> *Bless your heart, you work so hard*
> *to take care of me.*

Who did she think I was, who she called
Mama? I squandered the moment replaying
the words I'd always craved to hear, wondering
if she knew my name. Never mind
what you're called when love speaks. I should
have kissed her cheek and blessed her back—

> *Sugar Pie, my darling girl,*
> *I'd do anything for you.*

I Never Thought My Mother

would slip back in after she died.
    How astonishing that she's arrived

            as a copperhead living under the porch.
    I stand on the edge and scan the yard.

Mostly, I do not see her. But
    in August, nearing birthing, she eases

            onto the asphalt to let the sun
    soothe the cold from her scales. She coils

about the drain spout or stretches
    along the driveway's grass fringe.

            I know she is my mother because
    her slow unspooling beguiles me. I know

her because I can't take my eyes off her.
    I watch with that same stitch at my sternum—

            if I clear my mind of fear, we might
    reconcile. I suppress my need for her

embrace. I imagine I am not the one
    who needs escaping. At any moment,

her languid looping patterns could break
into lightning. My husband unlocks

the gun safe, warms up on a paper target.
        She cares nothing about death.

                She will return, one life to the next,
until I no longer need her.

III

809 Whitehall Road, Knoxville, Tennessee

Still there, the bois d'arc tree,
its thorns, its fallen green globes

> bleeding against the drive.
> There, the creek behind the house,

tadpoles sprouting frog legs.
Inside, my father's vacant desk —

> his books, his briefcase,
> his looping, leaning script.

Still, my mother demanding
once and never again:

> *Why did you leave him alone,*
> *not even a blanket to cover him?*

Me still running
across the empty lot for help.

> There, the dogwood, still,
> its lowest branch the right height

to climb up, hide from the world,
gossamer blossoms fluttering down.

Rondelet: Electra at Twenty

My father's dead.
Killed, unsung—what does it matter?
My father's dead.
Who's the new man in Mother's bed?
What it means to be this daughter—
grieve alone, seek vengeance after
my father's dead.

Rivals

after Stanley Kunitz

My mother never forgave me for being
the one who knelt beside my father,
my ear pressed, listening for his heart.
The list—the blanket, the ambulance—
all I could have done and did not—
hissed from her lips. If she could make
death my mistake, cast me out at last—

But she could not. His heart stopped;
he was mine. My hair billowed
like his, my arms and legs swung
to his rhythm, my heavy brows brooded
over hazel eyes—she would not
look at me. *Do you think you are
the only one who's lost someone?*

Did You Know Azalea Honey's Poisonous, Like Guilt?

Thud against the bumper
as the boxer bulleted into the road.
How slowly the breath heaved
as the dog's lungs filled,
how still as stones his eyes—
the flame, the subsequent dim wick.

Oh, to see what's coming!
The sleek shape flashing across the yard
toward the car, or my mother
ambling across the porch,
chattering, admiring the azaleas,
not minding her feet—
the missed step, the downward crumple
into a heap beside the barbecue,
a pile of laundry, arms and legs
askew in all directions.

If I see a boxer now, I cannot
fondle its ears or stroke its trembling flank.
The young cop's hand on my shoulder—
the dog running loose all year,
the owner warned and warned.

I should have warned my mother
about that step. Instead, I stood there

toting up the ways I'd failed.
Which was all I could seem
to do about the cataclysm of limbs
and lamentation at my feet,
that and hoist her up, that
and buckle her into the car for the ER.

The blossoms were already
beginning to drop, and there was
nothing I could to do stop them.

My father just home

from the war—Hawaiian girls, cigarettes, Midway
locked in his ditty box, the key dropped in the Pacific.
But not to stay. The GI bill, the lure of a college town—
the same endless wind-wrecked plain as home,
sky blackened by earth—but the world
so much wider.

          And there she is, his will-be wife,
my mother, not so foreign as the island girls
but glamorous—lipstick, sultry film star smile,
the tiny gap between her teeth an invitation, not like
the plain girl at home his mother mentioned every letter—
docile, modest in the front pew.

          The wedding—
pearls, magnolia blossoms, Gulf-damp heat—
the groom's sister crying, the bride's cousins smirking,
sipping at their pocket flasks, a bill shoved hard
along the bride's wrist into her sleeve, her mother's hiss:
Enough to get you home—you'll wake up and understand
the mistake you've made.

          The little slips of paper,
her mother's penned poisons tucked into my mother's
valise—shards among the stockings and chemises.

A man who owns nothing is nothing.
Don't look for me at your door.
Until now, you never disappointed me.

My father beside my mother in the car, her hand in his.
With the cash she buys him a gold band.

My Mother Wants to Know If Her Money's Holding Out

hunched   gray
                as an oncoming
                storm

her voice   a draft
                through a leaky window

It'll last as long as you need it   I tell her

        and then some

Are you lying

a voltage   in my throat

I lied to her once—   eleventh grade
                some contest
I did not want to enter

Daddy's voice   like the chill
                of a door
                locking—

Don't lie to your mother again

And I never have

                         she looks

like a weeping

        willow   wild

in the wind

        all confusion   and decrepit

beauty

for a heartbeat   that softest

part of us

the gods picked   to excise

finds us   divines us

Another Buoyancy

Not stones, not stalks, not fallen branches,
nor some disturbance of water by feeding fish.
On the far side of the glassy gray-brown river,

> a good forty geese flock in the shallows.
> They are stipple in a watercolor—reflection
> of the bank's green. Or a slow flux, bubbles

propelled by the slightest breath across water.
Even a parade of neon windmills, kayaks
wagging their blades, does not disturb them.

A wonder none of us ever drowned.
My mother laughing, telling the story
again—Gulf Coast summer heat,
the treacherous log flume,
the rush of brackish water,

> no lifeguard, no lessons, no ladder.

Swimming they called it,
she and her cousins, all boys,
though a panicked flail and gasp
was what it was. I could never
figure her laughter. I can't

imagine the ovum that with my father's thrust
would become this body, already there,

   a little moon shining in the night like a secret,
   a tiny pearl packed among her sisters, a world

emerging lucent from the face of the deep,
floating there in my mother's placid waters.

Electra at the River I

the swollen current sounds like distant traffic
            the swallow and slosh
     near the bank

on the few boulders left unsubmerged
        geese turn their elegant necks
               to the undersides of wings
        opened like blades

bare-chested boys in yellow and orange kayaks
         whoop and wave their paddles
      geese boys float together out of sight

the strangeness of a river
          turned brown by summer rains
            the unfathomed silences
      between mothers and daughters

again and again my mother
         her birthday her death day
     every year

she pronounced me strange for asking
       why there were no photographs
           of her wedding to my father
       dwelling on the past

or why after he died the only trace of him
                    was the faded wall
          where pictures had hung

around the bend the boys bellow
          a heron
                    or a colony of turtles

if they petition their earthly gods
                    if they beckon thus
          the spirits of animals

is it because

                              they grieve
          but have no words?

Under the Canopy of Night

Cool metal under bare feet
the pulse of ripples against the side
of a small boat.

A lantern burning on the bow.
                              A father

whispers to his young daughter,
reminds her to keep quiet as she can
not to scare the fish.

The small girl, the melody of the lake,
her father's stillness, the rocking.

Turtles, Late Summer

How lethargic these top-of-the-food-chain
lake dwellers. No one to hide from,
nothing to do, apparently, but breathe,
looking from shore like the ends of submerged sticks.
From above, straight down from the pier,
a garden of gray platters waits for dinner,
floating under the surface, hanging, it seems,
by their noses, from the air, four paddle-like feet,
snaky heads.
                    Along the trunk of a tree
fallen in water, a swarm of eleven dreadnaught
sun worshippers, the largest heliotrope bending
her neck sunward. What is it I want? That perfect
symmetry — the reflection made of sun and water?
The homely, the stolid made into a work of art?

Revision

Because after widowhood
and a second marriage,
you had five names,
(trochees linked by single stresses)

which you tried on
like skirts, blouses, jackets,
mixing and matching
according to your mood,
for different occasions,
a pile left on the closet floor—

three of the five for your license,
a different three for taxes,
yet another three for your will—

who but I to untangle the mess
when you were gone?

Because in the end
you left it to me to decide
who you were—what name
to display I meant to say—
on the two-person headstone,
bought so long ago,
half of which
had been blank for fifty years,

I made the last edit,
struck out the final trochee,
gave you back to Daddy,
God help you.

IV

Piano Lesson Triolet

At the keyboard, we nearly touch—
we're closer here than anywhere.
Her fine fingers, my shoulders hunched,
playing scales, oh, we almost touch.
Her hands alight, fly. If I could—
I paw the fastidious keys. There's
scant space between us. Will we touch?
We're closer here than anywhere.

At the Least Movement, the Whole Structure Collapses

after *The Palace at 4 A.M.*
— Albert Giacometti

At last, a marble statue
in her penultimate palace,
a Venus shorn of arms,

                immaculate, immune

      to embrace. What's left
      of her music, the long sigh
      of the erect spine.

The tower leans strangely
since the last disaster.
The long dead dove of peace

            arranged as if it might fly.

      And I am the floating glass,
      nearly invisible, hanging there,
      offering her reflection.

I look again. A chess piece
and a wooden backbone,
a pterodactyl fossil,

slender dowels, wire, string.

A surrealist vision made of air.
My mother isn't even there.

Mother of Roses

and clematis that vined the trellis near the pond
      and crepe myrtles that flared across the field

         where the barn leaned, hesitating
before the inevitable fall, rest now.

The choices have all been made. On the porch,
      where hummingbirds whirred at the red feeder,

         I waited for your verdict: *I'll take the rocker*
or *I'll need the smaller of the two dressers*.

What I dreaded: *I'm staying here after all.*
      Instead, you shrank in your chair like a child

         waiting for punishment, saying nothing.
When I was ten, and you might or might not

have even noticed, the neighborhood kids and I
      would haul out quilts, lay them over limbs,

         clothespin them into doorways, rooms.
Sometimes, one of us would die—the mouth

fallen open, head rolled to the side,
      eyes fixed, just like on *Rawhide*.

It never occurred to any of us to consider
the deceased's wishes for disposition of the body.

We waited for the sudden intake of air,
jumped up and played some new game.

In the bedroom, where you slept one week
on one side of the bed, one week on the other,

while the movers arrived with their dollies and boxes
and the blue walls bore the light from the window,

you lamented: *I was happier in this house
than anywhere else I have ever lived,*

then escaped to that half-lit corner
of your basement. I pointed to the loveseat,

the bedside table, the microwave, only
what would fit in the new place.

The new owners built a stable. The pond
dried up in drought, refilled in plentiful rain.

The barn finally fell, Queen Anne's lace
burgeoning among the tangled, twisted timbers.

A Plane Rises, Smaller, Smaller, into Clouds

1.
The man at Gate 44 makes of his body
a small cave—pitched forward in his seat,

elbows to knees, scowl aimed at his phone.
Nothing can touch him. It's not even a cave, really.

A crevice in limestone, a boulder's sliver of shelter.
Scant harbor against the evangelizing seatmate,

the missing flight crew, the terrorist with a fuse.
Meager shield against loss. He makes do.

2.
In Mesa Verde, refuge under the cliff's
edge, walls glow ochre in early sun—

the day's first stone-on-stone grinding
of corn, foot drums pounding in the Kiva.

Tucked deep into rock alcoves, dwellings
heaped from a dream of mortar, sandstone brick.

If you ask today why the ancestors left,
the answer is always: *It was time to go.*

3.

The day my father's heart gave out, I sought
asylum in the upper corner of the room

where the ceiling meets two walls. I rested there.
Then, I took repose in the window's sanctuary,

the hushed curtains hanging, the slant of evening
falling across the wall, so soundless, so inert.

The smoothness of the counterpane. The quiet
dust drifting through a column of light.

Burn Maybe Bones

we considered   the red velvet curtain   how neatly it hung
and maybe   my mother was rolled in   her weight
on the gurney   the color of light   through a window
her lids stitched   but not artfully   a rag doll sewn

in a hurry   and I thought it doesn't matter   maybe
I made myself   touch her cold cheek   and the flowers
over her heart   the shed petals   maybe someone opened
the veil   and we watched her enter   the murky oven

and I thought   *we're both safe now*   maybe I could
stand the grim inertia   only by thinking   *this body too is ash*
and looking   at my hands   and the hands
on the clock moved   and someone   told the man

to open the drape again   and he looked stern   and maybe
he glanced at me   opened it anyway   and the oven door
and it was red in there   maybe it was red   and if wood
is stacked too close   it will not burn   maybe bones too

must be stirred   and the man raked   and the little house
of my mother's ribs   collapsed   and her skull spun away
and I couldn't tell   one part from another   maybe I thought
that's where I come from   and the look on the man's face—

Lilacs

I sit at my desk, the bookshelf sagging with words.
You speak to me from the wooden coffin under the window.
The nightgown you wore as you died, the color of lilacs.
Your fragrance almost gone from it now.

You speak to me from the wooden coffin under the window.
I imagine you are the bank of fog settling over the mountain.
Lilacs. Your fragrance almost gone now.
I tracked your slowing pulse above your collarbone.

I imagine you have settled over the mountain.
Once, you said, *I don't want to go and leave you here alone.*
Your pulse slowed its beating above your collarbone.
Another day, you asked, *Why did you never love me?*

Once, you told me, *I don't want to leave you here alone.*
I'm at my desk, the bookshelf sagging with words.
Another day, you asked, *Why did you never love me?*
That nightgown you wore as you died, the color of lilacs.

Maestro

Hush and sweep of blade
                           along the strop,
my grandfather's plow-weary fingers
along the razor's spine, his supple, sun-worn,
work-weathered wrist.

Then, like the field's tasseling corn or sunrise,
a dearth of hurry, a languid circling,
                                  (the same
stirring as at the table, shuffling dominoes), soap
into lather,
               the silvertip badger bristles,
the smooth olive wood handle,
                           the porcelain mug,
the lavish meringue his one luxury.

Between leather and lavender, the scent,
and from his overalls,
                    the garden's aroma—
radish sting, earth. To his granddaughter,
a nod and a smile
                 that will last sixty years.
A radiance, a virtuosity of kindness revealed
stroke by stroke
               by the silver straightedge.

Electra at the River II

Feet aching with cold, I wade the shallows,
apprentice myself to a dragonfly waltzing
through her mansion of air. Shade crowds
among tree trunks. Once, I worshipped
the opulent bodies of otters, envied their
hidden sanctuary among roots and hollows.

Always the draw of water. At six I blinked—
sunlight flashing, a rippling mountain stream—
while my father rolled his pants legs. Crossing
then, we hopped wet stone to wet stone.
                                        That
last summer before he died, we devoted a boat
to a tame current. I sat facing him, an oar
in each hand like some mythic winged creature,
rowing, rowing backwards into the day.

Boundary II

Scrawny, long-armed, four-thumbed, the baby knuckle-walks down a green slope to a weedy patch; the silverback surveils — a mountain, massive, slack squat, focus of a samurai; the mother, twig in her mouth, glances from one to the other, vigilant, zoo born, jungle innocent. *Gorilla beringei beringei, endangered*. Familiar and strange at once, like driving past my childhood home after decades, after several owners: the man pulling weeds in the yard could be my father. When I was young, men spent afternoons like that — settled on their haunches, forearms draped over knees, old tobacco can for spitting, pocketknife for trimming nails. Some *enough*, some refusal of the rock wall before him, the silverback pivots, clambers up the slope on all fours, the mother turns and follows, then the baby, like the last straying lines of a parachute drawing in.

Snakes

Floating on the window glass: stun smudge,
breast and wing. Somewhere in the woods,
a wind whine—whistling space under an eave,
shed door ajar—somewhere in the woods,
they are unwinding, rising from furtive dens
into light, wide flat jaws heat seeking. The way
fear makes the world contract. If I could

expand into joy, I would. No one after me
will keep the Polaroid of the Chimney Tops—
my father took it, held it in his hand.
We carried pails into a thicket—
the blunt chime, blackberries against tin—
Mind where you step, they wait
for birds under the thorns. And now,

I check the old gaps—drain spout? stoop?
The ancestral birthplace under the porch:
coppery length along the driveway,
sine wave sunning on asphalt,
looped form under the ferns. The fantasy

of safety. The story he told—cotton field,
bag heavy on his shoulder, looking down
between his feet: the coil. On the trail that day—
the saddle-patterned skin, the arrow-shaped head
lifted, cocked—I inched carefully away,
the long body sliding slowly into shadow.

v

Electra at Seventy

Does every girl's passage into womanhood
begin with tragedy? Which of the gods prescribed

that sequence? A rectangle pops up on Ancestry.com,
the cursor blinking, blinking as if to console:

Take as long as you like to answer.
My father's name, birthplace, two choices:

Living? Deceased? Next to Living, a green dot stares,
already supplied, as if to say *just go with it, let him*

be alive, albeit grayer, thinner, a bit of a stoop,
still the same briefcase in his hand. All this time

he barely notices when I confront him. Or he
ignores me, can't be bothered with grief.

All this time has he been alive? "Death in the Bath"
a scene he played before he made his escape

to the other life, the other family? Rage roars up
from my gut with its bloody claw. He can't be

Living. I click Deceased.
I click it again.

Landscape with Ash

Mountains at dawn through the window,

inkblot

in the fold between one peak and another. Morning
enigma, a density of granite or gravity, maybe

the black spill of sorrow —

obscure in the world's

brightness. Cleaning the Thanksgiving oven, I remember
in the novel I am reading, a father gives his son

a biscuit smudged with ash, tells him nothing is cleaner
than ash.

You are strange, Mother said, *dwelling on the past.*
Last night, I found a hidden stairway leading down

into a maze of rooms—familiar (what treasure had I
forgotten there, what jewel left behind?). Too many sofas,
no lamps, books spilling out of broken boxes.

The bread

of atonement —what the father said as he offered his son
the ashy biscuit.

Consider the dusty corners, the gritty
baseboards—they will never be clean all at once. No point

in trying. Simply address the napkin's cranberry stain,
the gray amoeba

        of coffee on the kitchen floor.
Paying attention to dreams, Mother told me, *a waste.*

Enough

In this heat, a body decomposes fast.
Last week, a squirrel lay dead beside the pool.
The thing we fear consumes us at the last.

My heart sank, thinking of the gruesome task,
but off I went in search of the right tool.
In this heat, a body decomposes fast.

When I returned, I saw, taken aback,
maggots teeming, feeding, heaving. Who'll
deny our fear consumes us at the last?

Later, nothing but a damp, grey mass
no longer recognizable as squirrel.
In this heat, a body decomposes fast.

I looked today (the sky was overcast).
Nothing left but spectral spine, perfect skull.
The thing we feared consumed us at the last.

Perhaps you've had enough of death? you ask.
Enough indulgence in the catacombs? You'll
agree, a body decomposes fast.
What we keep secret often shows up last.

Taco Tuesday

Maybe this is mirage, this belonging,
grandbaby on my shoulder, eighteen days,
already hoisting up her wobbly head,
daughter in the kitchen shredding chicken,
older grandkids showing me their homework
or downstairs playing foosball, husband still
here after all the ways I've maimed him,

or maybe the mirage was that concrete curb
where I crouched—my own arms curled about me,
fetal, a personal geometry of wretchedness—
or maybe the jagged scar on my belly
where something red and squalling and helpless
was taken out but not a baby, no one
telling me *Push Push Push*.

The Potted Jade

My husband can't stay awake. Nightly,
            amid the sonorous breathing, I read
                        my phone like scripture, looking for God—
                                    photos of empty streets post-rapture,

graphs like talus slopes of ascending death.
            Relentless. After breakfast, his eyelids sag.
                        I find him snoring on the couch.
                                    An orgy of sleep.

I inflate into every crevice of the house,
            the walls bending imperceptibly as I inhale,
                        straightening again on the exhale.
                                    His chin stubbles. His mail piles up. I bleach

doorknobs, the espresso machine. Daytime,
            I plot the topology of the potted jade;
                        at night, the room's reflection in black
                                    window glass: lamp, table, woman in a chair.

Outside, under a fracture of moon, the copperheads
            coil in their dens, deep in winter's dream.
                        Even the bullfrogs, their blood nearly dimmed,
                                    drowse, doze under their blanket of ice.

Quantum Physics

I know precisely what he will order
from any menu. As well as
his latitude, his angle of repose, his f-stop.
His warm hands? I'm crazy about them.
And his mechanics, his partial differentials.
A koala, or some other nocturnal animal,
he sleeps draped in the armpit of a tree.
His smooth shaved head, his high peaks,
his swollen snowmelt streams,
I rely on them, and his library of lost saints.
He wears socks with his sandals. He kneels,
pollen dusted, before the first daffodil.

Forty-Ninth Year of a Marriage

Delicate Planets—three hydrangea blossoms floating
in a crystal bowl. Soft light sings from their petals.

All spring we studied masks, dreamed of vaccines,
bleached handles, packages we gathered curbside.

But now, in summer's lull, he has cut these three—
the big blue one pulses out its name, *War with Death*;

the bluish purple I call *Precision of the Present Moment*;
the otherworldly green tinged with mauve I think of as

Impermanence of all Things. Despite the certainty
that we will die, one of us before the other, one of us

almost surely left to orbit out of kilter, alone,
he has placed on the table between us this light.

Boundary III

The looping muscled form   hour-glass skin
the awful sentience   centered   in the coil
the elegant neck's exquisite turn   wide flat jaw
narrowing to arrow   copperhead.   Big as a plate
she suns beside the step.   Anyone would hug
the porch's farthest possible edge   watch for tensing
a trigger cocking   search her eyes   those vertical
slitted pupils.   *If she'd return my gaze*—   She never
moves.   After she's gone   for weeks in dreams
her spools unleash   launch that lethal head
those harrowing fangs.   By night   slithering six-inch
sine waves   her babies   swim in the streaming street.
By day   the shaded yard   every fallen leaf
every dappled pattern   in the mulch   every patch
of flattened grass   transfixes.   The beauty
its terrible   proximity.

Cahokia

I don't know how to be a vessel. When my mother's father
drank himself to death, she was a day's bus ride away
at school, got the news by telegram.
$\qquad\qquad\qquad\qquad\qquad$ She told that story
once and never again. Today, in my dead mother's yard,

fog—you could forget the elms had ever been there.
Bulldozing in the 60s along the Mississippi, workers
dug up pots, beads, shells,
$\qquad\qquad\qquad\qquad$ remains of Cahokia,
a city as large in the 13th century as London was—

plazas, mounds, courtyards, towers.
$\qquad\qquad\qquad\qquad\qquad$ Imagine getting
to work with your backhoes, blueprints, federal funding
only to find someone else had been there first.
At the end of her life, my grandmother made my mother

promise to keep the stacks of funeral visitation books,
proof the forgotten ancestors had been somebody.
Today, thinking of my daughters, I snap a photo
of every page of each decrepit, dusty book and heave

them into the dumpster with the mouse-ridden sofa.
In Cahokia, the Mississippians built a wood henge
to mark the sun's solstice.

Now, the sun burns away
the fog and across the valley, Flat Top Mountain smolders

in autumn light. I don't know where in these woods
the copperheads are winding in their dens,

                                where
the turkeys are fattening on acorns, their necks ratcheting
down and up. If I knew how to tell you that, I would.

The Last Dust Swept Away

after *Sun in an Empty Room, 1963*
—Edward Hopper

It feels like the sun is passing
over the blank face
of a dry canyon where nothing lives,

slicing down hard and yellow,
carving its geometries
across the rock.

But there isn't a desert
for a thousand miles.

Through the window, crepe myrtle
blazes, blooming beside a pond.

So much is missing.

Soon, you will no longer know who I am,
the room, scraped of every trace of you.

Lunaria

To make that trip again across the Appalachians.
To set off at dawn, early spring,

make my way under the rising slivered crescent,
among the mountains' stooped shoulders.

First blush in the crowns of redbuds.
Icicles dripping from road-cut schist.

When I arrive, she's in the garden, as she was.
No diagnosis, no documents of surrender.

Only the smell of spring mud from the pond.
Tender buds of cattails, yellow forsythia.

She knows me—not the wrench
come to dismantle her life, but her child.

Her hands are full of the waste of winter,
cut stalks—yarrow, thistle—at her feet.

Then, between the leather of her thumb and
forefinger, she rubs the seedpods of moon plant,

teaches me to strip the dry husks,
let the lucent disks shine like silver.

Acknowledgments

Thank you to the editors of the journals in which these poems first appeared, sometimes in earlier versions.

Abandon Journal: "Electra at the River I," "Landscape with Ash"

Asheville Poetry Review: "Enough"

Cider Press Review: "Another Buoyancy"

The Comstock Review: "Dead Five Years," "Rondelet: Electra at Twenty"

Crosswinds Poetry Journal: "February"

Delmarva Review: "Revision"

Five Points: A Journal of Literature & Art: "I Never Thought My Mother"

The Great Smokies Review: "Boundary III"

Kakalak: "Lunaria," "Maestro"

LEON Literary Review: "Quantum Physics"

New Ohio Review: "Cahokia"

North Dakota Quarterly: "Burn, Maybe Bone"

The Poeming Pigeon: "Forty-Ninth Year of a Marriage"

Redheaded Stepchild: "A Plane Rises, Smaller, Smaller, into Clouds"

Rogue Agent: "Taco Tuesday"

Southern Poetry Review: "Electra at the River II"

Tar River Poetry: "Eclipse," "How to Unknot a Straitjacket,"
   "The Last Thing She Ever Said to Me," "Unsummoned"

Twelve Mile Review: "Doily"

US 1 Worksheets: "Under the Canopy of Night"

Valparaiso Poetry Review: "Easter Sunday, 1956"

Vita Poetica: "Our Lady of the Locked Unit"

These poems owe tribute as follows: "Doily" to Ellen Bryant Voigt, "My Mother Dead Five Years" to Martha Rhodes, and "I Never Thought My Mother" to Jack Gilbert. The collection's title is borrowed from a line in Ellen Bryant Voigt's poem "Maestro."

Thank you to my many teachers, especially Marianne Boruch, Sally Ball, Sally Keith, and Martha Rhodes. Thank you to the many people who have supported this work with their tireless reading, critique and enthusiasm, especially Karen Hildebrand, Whitney Waters, Eric Nelson, and Jeffrey Levine. Thank you to Diane Lockward for her generosity and clarity. Thank you to my parents, who loved me. And thank you to my husband, Bruce, for his unflagging patience and for always believing in me.

About the Author

Kathy Nelson is the author of two chapbooks, *Cattails* (Main Street Rag, 2013) and *Whose Names Have Slipped Away* (Finishing Line Press, 2017). The recipient of the 2019 James Dickey Prize from *Five Points: A Journal of Literature & Art*, she holds an MFA in poetry from the Warren Wilson Program for Writers. Her work has appeared in *The Practicing Poet: Honing the Craft* and in numerous journals, including *LEON Literary Journal*, *New Ohio Review*, *Southern Poetry Review*, *Tar River Poetry*, and *Valparaiso Poetry Review*. She has worked as a teacher, telecommunications engineer, and chaplain. She lives in Nevada.

www.kathynelsonpoet.com

CPSIA information can be obtained
at www.ICGtesting.com
Printed in the USA
BVHW042328110723
667085BV00002B/26